Plague Animals

Plague Animals

Rebecca Edwards

PUNCHER & WATTMANN

First published in 2021
Published by Puncher and Wattmann
PO Box 279
Waratah NSW 2298

http://www.puncherandwattmann.com
puncherandwattmann@bigpond.com

NATIONAL
LIBRARY
OF AUSTRALIA

A catalogue entry for this book is available from the National Library of Australia.

ISBN   9781925780772

Cover design by Miranda Douglas
Typesetting by Morgan Arnett
Printed by Lightning Source International

Contents

Nikko; Almost Like Love at First Sight

for my daughters
Miriam and Amelia

Manifesto

The Exile of the Imagination

"More remote, I fear, my place of exile
Than storied ones in lands beyond the seas."
Murasaki Shikibu

Daybirds settle down now, in holes in spotted gums
in thicketed lantana
in the leaf-matted snug of a burrawang's outspread wing.
The galahs have walked their sunset crests across paddocks,
ducks have skidded onto the dam's runway, and rowed themselves
to shore.
Magpies have inspected the new-wired fence
and the floor of the shed.
Blue-wrens have talked their thumb-nail wives to sleep.

Now the mopoke gathers the feathercloak of the forest around her.
Now black calves sleep beside their mothers, inside the electrified fence.
I wish you, Rosemary, a night of sleep.
I wish you this burrawang-feathered bush, cycads dancing
through cross-hatched night, spreading their fronds low over seeds
    smooth as eggs.
I wish you the burrawangs' slow spiraling growth
along the steep banks of the Shoalhaven.

Under its tuft of shaggy moss a centipede curls in on itself, waiting
    out day.
When night comes, let that armoured sleeper catch all your sorrows
and break them open,
reduce them to chitin and wings.
Let him tunnel through forests of moss, on the flank of a broad grey
    stone.
Let orchids inch their yellow roots into a niche,
let fig roots prise boulder from cliff-face,
let a wombat emerge from earth-scented sleep and scratch herself awake.

The lyrebird is dancing on his mound.
The cycads are dancing on their stony trunks.
The lovers sleep in their nest of earth, under the gum, hip cradling hip
forever.

St George Mapping Exercise (from the sketchbook of Merric Boyd)
Life Holds Me Through all Eternity
love for all stays with me to give
now I am Merric floating
in Every Purpose truth
Governs Perfect Love All Day
and Resting at Night. Now
Sweet Music is my intelligent Life for
all Day Amen.

Across the river, those famous rocks, stooping like wombats to drink.
This side, the Shoalhaven scoops white sand into banks and beaches.
Lowtide crows press their prints across glistening sandbars.
Coals of an old fire sink into windblown drifts,
lantana twists its sweetsmelling ropes over itself,
weaving a basket of blossom and thorns.
Wombats breathe deep in their burrows,
bodies grey as Hunter Valley sandstone
fur beaded with tick-eggs and sand.

I walked, a sand-coloured woman, along the bank.
Yellow flycatchers hopped closer to take me to task, for brushing too
    close to their nests.
High-up from the tideline, I stepped over a log, and found in its roots
the bruised silver of a fish.
Who had flipped it out of the river and left it?
Was it dry enough to take, or would it stink
and break open?
But its mouth gasped at my touch, and its tail batted the air.
In my hand the fish gulped its element

righted itself
finned down the ramp of my fingers
and followed its shadow into dark water.

In that mad basket that the stars are weaving
what if my whole purpose were simply this: to find that fish
to put it back into its life
to walk on again, down the track wombats had trodden
not for me,
not for any human need at all.

Poetry and Me

Poetry is my father's tobacco breath and his deep voice chanting in the night-weirded room: *We are the hollow men/ we are the stuffed men/ leaning together/ headpiece filled with straw* and though we chant over him for a proper bed-time story the rhythms of poetry are seeded in our brains, the scratching of the rats' feet in our dry cellar and the hickory dickory dock of the hurrying mouse and What's that by your trough, Mister Pugh?
at the kitchen table, my mother answering herself: *Pigs can't talk dear (sneering) I know one who can*
poetry is a joke that gets better at each telling is predictable as the egg in its china cup is startling as the scalping of a small bald man
and Joan Baez is a magpie singing because there is dew on the grass this morning, singing so that worms rise naked and weeping out of the earth but Bob Dylan is not any kind of bird, is barefoot dancing on an unsealed quartz-tooth road
She loves you yeah yeah yeah is not poetry. Poetry never had to rhyme never has to tell you anything never really repeats a single word or line.
Poetry is the hard work of drafting and poetry is the little gift of a song.
Poetry is instead of love. I was thirteen when poetry said 'Jump!' but the steps were only second-storey high.
Poetry squints at me cocks its head to one side says 'Snap out of it!' dances me over the cliff says 'I know you are afraid of heights but look at this.' Poetry never said that everything would be alright.
Poetry is my mother's hand stroking my hair, her voice quavering *Luna appears in the sky* poetry is that ancient moon
and poetry is my daughter humming in her cot to *rockabye baby on the treetop/ when the wind blows the cradle will rock*
a song spiralling from the navel of a small pink elephant
and from the lips of her monkey-mother
and if the bough breaks as she tumbles into language
poetry will catch her when she falls

Harvest Song

I grew like magic I grew a tail then ate it up inside me.
Before I was born I lived a whole life in the womb.
That was the first time I died
when I was delivered from my mother into my mother's arms.
That was the day the colour of my eyes began to change.
I knew the history of the earth because I was inside it
The worm I
ate the fish I
ate the dinosaursharkfrogbear.
All the cells in my body danced in the gut of a beetle
danced in the antennae of a snail
danced in a whirlpool on the sun
danced in the dust in the corner
of a sigh.
I heard fragments of song and unstrung lines of music.
I heard the footprint of a city
uncoiling from a knot inside my spine.
I put my lips to the meniscus on the face of the universe.
I took a breath.

The Crows

The crows have found the dead crow in the garden.
I exposed him today to the sun
and the sharp-eyed crows have found him

now they are calling round the house
angry and sad
at this hollow-eyed brother

they are chanting the death-chant
all together
tossing their words
from throat to throat

I wish I could tell them
that I didn't kill him
but it's not true

I took his death in my hands
when I wrapped him in my jacket
and brought him home.

The crows are dancing their outrage in the garden:
who is this?
who is this brother?
while he lies there in his musty feathers
with the white mould on his skin.

I wanted those bones
I wanted those brilliant wings
I wanted to dance, like a shaman
with the words in my throat like amulets
and my hands on fire

the crows are shouting
get up! get up out of the ground!
and when they fly over the rooftops
the shadow-bird flies with them
and they have finished with the corpse.

The Young Milton Moon

Sometimes you get tired of giving it away.
Of lovers expecting gifts of your life's work.
If you were an architect
would they ask you to build them a house?
Not just design, but *build*: scrape each brick out of the clay
you scrub pub toilets to afford.

Sunday mornings are good.
Football drunks drop coins into their piss,
stumble off with open flies.
Why are you doing this?
You're almost thirty.
See that derro who won't look you in the eye:
that's you. Just give it time.

It's getting colder.
A skinny girl with goosebumps on her arms jogs by
dragging a panting dog: *'Come on!'*
If you were a dog the other dogs
wouldn't stoop to sniff your arse.

They're not just pots they're vessels into which you've poured your guts;
canopic jars of this country's earth and your own.
Scrub your hands under the tap and walk home.

They're waiting for you, your people, tall as gums,
generous as figs.
They have passed through fire.
No mongrel wanted to buy even one,
and you kept your prices low.

You can still smell vomit and piss.
Who told you you were any good?

Across at West End a barge claws the river deeper,
more dangerous.
A mean moon snickers as you throw them all in.
They slip under without even a splash
so you smash one on the footpath and chuck in the shards.
No one's getting any more for free.

After Seven Centuries

Jakarta, 2008

He was killed a week before the armistice.
She looks across the city through windows sealed shut.
He worked in poverty as an illustrator and engraver.
She counts twenty-seven mosques
His criticism has been influential.
domes individual as breasts.
He wrote a small body of poetry in his twenties before going mad.
She buys twelve crickets in a plastic bag.
He dominated the literary life of his time from an early age.
The crickets crawl across the tiles scenting water
He set out to write a poem in every known form.
they find the kitchen and start to sing.
She worked intermittently as a teacher and governess.
'God is great!' they shrill from folds in the curtains.
From 1837 he was confined to mental asylums.
'God loves us, His crickets, and has brought us to this place.'
He earned a frugal living as a writer and painter.
Sketching a rainforest in cricket cantata.
He was subject to depression and lived quietly in the country,
They kill each other by biting just behind the head
cared for by friends.
littering her floor with wings and legs.
He died in a tavern quarrel.
The muezzins are stridulating from their towers.
He was in and out of favour at the court.
She draws the curtains.
His poetry was published after his death.
'Thank you thank you thank you for my instrument.'
Nothing certain is known about her life.

The Boat Builders of Gili Trawangan

That year he gave her an island for her birthday. It was hers
for five days. She trailed the cuffs of her trousers in the brimming
water. Each morning, while he was sleeping, she went to see what the
sea had brought her. Coral lumps washed up by storms and moulded
by a city of builders, as if they had dreamed of shapes they might
become on land: branches, antlers, mushrooms, mammalian brains.
She saw her eyes and her sex in the cowry's grin, her hair in tangled
line and her veins in torn nets wrapped around the mangroves'
polished roots. High up on a beach she found the boat builders. They
spoke to her in their language, pleased that she had come up to them,
coaxing her as if they knew her for a strange, shy bird. She would
have trusted their smiles to carry her from island to island. Their
hands were like boat-wood, clean, honest, hardened to a lifetime of
work. They offered her a seat on a stack of timber, as if she were a
guest or a treasured child, their eyes shining like pieces of polished
shell. The boat was a long, ribbed outline, a potential, a sketch in
honey-coloured wood. Time, thousands of years of it, flowed through
the timber, the island, the sea, and the boat-builders' hands, into the
woman's rib-cage, and into the rib-cage of the boat. A pause, a few
words exchanged in a language she hardly knew, and then she was
gone, out of that moment in the sun.

Cranky Poem

I don't like abstract nouns like *gravitas* or *lucidity*
at least not in a poem. Give me a sound, like *crunch,*
give me *dignity,* if you mean *dignity,* better still: describe the raptor's
wheeling flight over stubble sharpened to a field of needles in midday
    heat.
Are you clear on this? Can you find rapture in clarity of thought or style,
can you describe Claude Lorraine's lemon wash of sunset, flex
your paper avatars in plain English, ornate vernacular, a wrought-iron
    verandah,
brown-skinned batsman stepping up to the crease. The *thwock* of
    tight-wound ball of rubber
on crafted willow, white teeth glinting under the mushroom cap:
    HOWZAT!!!

August

When I'm old – but you didn't get to be old, Osip Mandelstam –
you got a berth instead on a black iron train.
Dark branches scratched against the sky
white as amnesia.

What had you done?
Why were you so dangerous?
Did you have to write that poem about a nose,
how it couldn't be trusted?

They sniffed you out at once, the wolf-pack
in their numberless coats.
Winter came knocking at your door.

Something to be said, after all,
to be born in a country not known for devouring its children.
Hard to be a poet in Australia, another young man once said
but not hard like your bare hand on the ice.

My she-wolf was kind autumn,
And August smiled on me – the month of the Caesars.

When I'm old, may even my sadness shine.

Quotations are from Osip Mandelstam ('Herds of Horses Whinny and Graze') except
for the line 'Hard to be a poet in Australia,' which is Michael Dransfield's.

For Mohammad Ali Maleki

Detained on Manus Island

1.
I am writing to you, man in a cage
because I heard you cry out
because I know about cages.

I brought armfuls of wattle today, sweet and lovely
for a bird who was hatched in captivity
who won't live long outside.
But how terrible, to clip her wings like this!

I didn't ask for
this decorative prisoner
rasping cuttlebone with her sensitive beak
calling after a passing drift of cockatoos.
The peppercorn eye considers me warily.
She nibbles my lip, chirruping softly
little hand-me-down guest.

What am I meant to do with her?
To set her free would be another kind of crime.

She's brought a mirror with her.
I see how a mind might be
let out of its trap:
not hateful or unclean
only strange and
in need of comforting.

2.
Meanwhile you remain
far away and in darkness.
We only hear about you
when a neck cracks against a rope
or when the north wind brings a faint howling
a dark smell.
The troubles that dislodged you from your country
squeeze into ten minutes of newsfeed
we tap our tongues against the roof of our mouths rapidly
scatter sorries like seeds.

Savage flowers, orange and black, stinking of rotten meat
how outraged we are to find them crouching
on the borders of our garden, spoor hidden in folds of clothing
and skin.

3.
Yesterday I strolled along the aisles of a Sunday market, humming
under the apple sun, rummaging with my daughter in a suitcase full
of books. A friendly haggle with the vendor interrupted - 'I'd better
deal with this —' we turned towards a group of women, a child in a pram.
'I'm just doing what I thought was right', a brick-faced woman
blustered, phone still aimed at bright scarves pinned with butterflies
and rhinestones, unhappy oval faces, an elegantly unfurled hand.
'She's filming us. She says that we have stolen from you.'
'No no, they've paid already,' the bookseller said, but still she waved
her phone: 'I was *concerned.*'
'In our religion, stealing is forbidden,' someone started, but the clouds
tiptoed closer, rain spatted on the pram's plastic cover, we had to pack
it in.

4.
You washed up on the wrong shoreline
finding wardens where you sought a garden.
We shake our heads, fold our arms
look down at the sand.
Only the drowned receive
the boundless plains.

Maleki's poetry collection, Truth in the Cage, was published by Verity La in 2017

Shaman at Vinnies

Fortitude Valley, Brisbane 2003

Cracked mannequins watch him
with shallow, flaking eyes
and we watch too
from the smoko steps
brown baked tiles
that have borne so many transactions.

Kevin has holes in his palms
from some old crucifixion
he tells me
he'll never be well again
that this morning
it was cruel to put his feet to the floor.

The shaman stalks by
shirt blue as smoke
hand swollen around the staff
planted in the footpath
with each sneakered step.

Not often you see a shaman
even at St Vincent's
where trannies try on spangles and wings
shuffling through the racks of shabby bargains.

Not often you see a man
feathers plaited in his beard
crystals slung around his thin blue neck
crying in the bric-a-brac section.

Kevin stubs out his cigarette on the bricks and sighs
'Well, it's a reason to get out of bed in the morning'

goes to serve the man
whose visions are a form of illness
who won't be asked to heal anybody
least of all himself.

Letter to The Crooked Little Finger

The woolly rhinos are gone, and the cave lions
who hunted you in spring.
Ice is restricted to one season - a few short months
and the mountain has folded itself
over the mouth of your cave.
We had forgotten about you, except in dreams.

Did you climb there in winter, when the giant bears slept
or in summer, when they foraged far from that place?
Did you know great words to soothe them
the first mark-makers
sharpening their claws on black stone?

You knew it was their place.
You set a skull on a plinth
facing the entrance
Ursus spelaeus, gnawer upon old bones
stares at rock that came down 20,000 years ago
cleaving the cave from light.

There are no paintings in this first chamber
only the skull and
at the very back
a stone where one man put his palm-print:
the right hand, a crooked little finger,
thirty-five signatures in ochre.

Thirty-five times, you came here
or killed thirty-five times; men or mammoths
horses, hyenas, antelope
or thirty-five of the masterpieces were painted by you
an individual at least six foot tall
whose positive hand-print

with its distinctive little finger
can be found deeper within the system of caves.

In this gallery, footprints pressed in soft, dry dust
by men and women who swiped their torches *here*
and *here* in long, black strokes of carbon
mingle with the claw-fringed pads of bears.
Here, a human child
is stalked or guided by a wolf.
Neither are hurrying.

Each chamber is a held breath,
a brush poised in mid-stroke.
A paleoarcheologist notes an animal response:
the back of his neck prickling
and an art historian feels *as though*
she has just disturbed the artists at their work.
Geologists who map the cave
in laserpoint 3D
awake from dreams where they are spoken to by lions.

The speckled panther, the aurochs
the little rhino with the big horn
the pair of rhinoceros in rut
the stiff-maned horse
the lion rubbing her flank
against the flank of her mate
the lion who sits on her sex and growls
the herds and prides
gathered at their waterhole -

you would not believe
what has become of them.

Yesterday
you scraped limestone back to its pale core
preparing a surface
for finger-brushed ochre and charcoal
each stroke a perfect line,
an embodiment
of the beast you asked to walk into your mind.
You reached up and pressed your open hand against the wall
there, where others had pressed their hand-prints
then stepped back
wiping ochre from your palm.

You turned to follow the thread of a torch
through flickering galleries
tunnels and archways of glistening calcite
pockets of cold, black air
until you came to the place where stars spun their little lights
around the silhouette of a skull

and you stepped out of the cave.

This poem was written after watching Werner Herzog's 2010 documentary, *Cave of Forgotten Dreams*, about paleolithic paintings discovered in the Chauvet –Pont d'Arc Cave in Southern France in 1994. The oldest are believed to be about 32,000 years old. Phrases in italics are quoted from the documentary.

Manifesto

All I had was a pen, and a pad of cheap, blue-lined paper.
All I had was *Cold Mountain*, and a bag of flat, grey stones.
When it rained, ink sank into the paper and stained the next page green.
I left my tongue-and-grooved room
I left the guavas ripening above the patio
I left the golden orb-weavers catching droplets of music in their webs.
I walked down the steps onto Charlotte Street.
All I had were Chris's last words: *You're not a feminist*
and a bachelor of arts.
All I had was the rage which drove my wrists onto metal-spiked gates
      at the City Gardens.
All I had was this stubbornness for language.
If they could have opened my head they would have found an entire
    poem
by John Donne: a compass and talisman against loss.
They would have found a shark-embryo
beating inside a spiral staircase envelope
and fifteen hundred Chinese ideograms, each a synonym for *futility*.
If they could have opened my head I would have left myself gladly
I would have swum away into the darkest unspoken ocean.
But instead, all I had were words, blunt, maiming arsenals
destroying *the thing of it* in my mouth
destroying every thing.

I left the room under the house on Vulture Street.
I took driftwood and a drawing: a girl running through a forest of blue
    trees.
I took the kitten that never learned to be clean.
I took Leonard Cohen's *cold and very broken*
I took the embryo that demanded ultrasound lullabies
in a brick half-house in Beenleigh.
All I had was loneliness dark-green as our bedsheets
spherical as the butcherbird's dawn-song

deep as the sky behind the powerlines
unassailable as that sky.
In two years I would find a name for it;
I no longer had to hide how often I washed my hands.
But I was never in it for the names, or even *a name*
a nest in the shelf at the back of the bookshop
the shelf marked POVERTY: DO NOT BUY.

All I have are breastfeathers of galahs, pink as dry summer grasses
and paddocks of tall dry grasses, then the shock of the Tumut River
tourmaline, spiritual descendent of snow.

Cold Mountain by T'ang poet Han Shan

Self Help and Poetry

Give me a life

focused and compact
flight-muscles tethered to hollow bones.

Give me the essence of song:
the perfect pitch of the butcherbird
the kookaburra's mad howl.

Give me the golden eyes of a currawong,
centre me to a wishbone
crucify me on the sky.

Or give me the crow's lice-ridden wings,
a pigeon's concrete plumage
the ibis's nicotine-yellow tail.

Let me squabble for garbage at the municipal tip.
Let me migrate out of this skin.

I'll give you a raging IQ and vertigo
my monkey heart and hands.
Yes, I'll give you my hands. Both of them.

Just open this cage.
(A mopoke's eye snaps open.)
Just disarm this skull.

Rimbaud in Bali

Candidasa 2019

After reading Rimbaud in Java: the Lost Voyage, *by Jamie James*

i
I hope you drown in your own vomit
you arrogant little shit
you overgrown schoolboy
run amok with gin
you little fucker
home-wrecker
you thief
you boring little turd
when you find the white sand beach
I hope you love it
with all your plastic heart

ii
at night the petrol tankers
shine like citadels
fairy palaces
under a fading moon
black sand
black sea
hermit crabs feasting on human shit &
black bones

nappies, a child's shoe, plastic cups, bubbles and beads of
styrofoam, lightbulbs, part of a watch-
 hibiscus, spear-tree of coastal australians, drops a
flower-cup onto the pile.
in the evening the people come to bathe
in the shabby water
women here and men
over there

three boys make a laughing boat
paddle it out to the breakers
where it falls apart
hilariously

long-legged hens shepherd clockwork fluff
towards the rubbish cornucopia
rake smoking plastic with dinosaur claws

you saw all this, didn't you
through absinthe sunglasses: the crocodile tankers
the carriages on the highways of the sky.

and I saw you
haunted in the forest
saw your tongue grow long
and wings burst from your shoulder-blades

the last wild orangutan
returning from extinction
picked lice from your beard &
suckled you at her breast.

you deserted the dutch army & poetry
ran wordless into a blue pool
felt the feet of the rice-planters
sink through your silky mud

which means everything & nothing
smoke from a clay pipe & smoke from the belly-up mountain
running in dog-dreams
eyes sprouted from the top of your head

iii
gak tahu
gak tahu mau
gak tahu apapun

gak mau
gak mau tahu
gak mau apapun

bau
gak bau
Pak Bau sits on a mossy stone
& smokes a gamelan of cigarettes

so it was that they never caught you
flying along the northern coast
in a horsehair mask & dorsal fin
a cloud in the shape of a man
a blue cloud
perfume in the cemetery

so it was that to touch you
was to bring out black bruises
on the heart, that bluish muscle

so it was that promises tinkled like footsteps
of ocean on skirts of white coral
so it was that you never returned

Operculum

A bridge, a spectator, a foreigner. A stranger. An observer. An umpire
a counselor, a set of ears.
A net stretched between two poles. A facilitator
a relaying station a spy.
Does she trust me or not?
Do I trust myself?
Can I trust him?
He is a proud and noble rabbit but I am also a rabbit and proud.
She is a princess a downpour a hurricane. She calls me from Singapore
and asks me have I seen him? Did she think I was seeing him? I didn't
    recognise the number I didn't take the call.
A bridge that falls down sometimes that lies down in the water.
I call back I answer her anxiety from the archipelago
he has gone missing.
I was meant to meet him I let myself be unavailable.
I am aloof I am a loner I am not a good transmitter
I said I must dine with my husband I said to my husband I must meet
    with this man.
I do not like my own company. I am not comfortable in my skin.
Should I be honoured should I be wary
what am I being offered what am I required to give?
If I am a door I am closed if a woman I am on the other side of the door.
He is missing he is not replying sometimes he does silly things
like sleeping with a woman he is not in love with
I am not in love with I am not the best of friends.
I am too lonely.
There was a man ready to weep in a garden
but my car was waiting and I ran.

Spider Lily

Small brown leaves drop quietly
from the fig outside my window
frangipani release their scent
cool and fresh and white
as the moon just passed its full, and rising.

These are the nights when I would go out looking.
The mirror told me that tonight I would find him
each dusk expectant as a spider lily, petal tips pressed together
ready to spring open just at that second when electric blue
darkens to indigo.

When I came home there was smoke knotted in my hair
and my self, a small boat, swamped on an alcoholic sea.
I didn't know where else to look
I didn't know how to ask them for a husband
or at least a dance.

It's good how something seems to spring back inside me
not like a flower; uncrushed
not like a spider lily.

The Hump

It begins as an itch
a shoot, striking from my left shoulder.
The left hemisphere
of the planet inside my skull
itches too
pulled by a misshapen moon.

It grows
meat and bone and sinew
a sail, a fin
fusing with my spinal column.
I bend to accommodate it.

It throws its arms around my neck
like the old man of the sea
or an abandoned child.
It whispers in my ear:
You're not good enough.
You will never be good enough.
You will never get rid of me.

It climbs inside my blood
corrosive as cancer
black as nicotine.
It can't be cut away
or tricked; it has its own
wolf track to the substation.

It flicks switches. It cuts things.
It cries me to sleep.

Trade

I'll trade my shadow
for a pocketful of pills
but do I have to give up this music?
Be brave, they tell me
prescribing chemicals
to lullaby demons
be strong, you tell me
mistaking tears for weakness.

In the garden, struggling with damp washing
I fight myself
with myself
alone.
If I succeed
no-one will recognise
how vast it was, how violent
If I fail
no-one will be surprised.

The song that travels through me
invisibly and unrecorded
is trapped in the same net
as my nightmares.

If pain sings,
if what I am doing when my hands are still and panic floods me
is shaking with the birth of a new music
then what I have submitted to
is an abortion.

A sweet smell comes from the chimneys
where they manufacture normalcy
in bitter, daily communions.

In their sedated womb
the conjoined twins sleep
arms around each other
mouths stuffed with cotton wool.

The surgeon assures me
they will feel nothing.
She holds up a delicate saw
strung with a single wire.
Begins.

Self Help and Poetry

Yesterday I wanted to cut off my hands
and I could've done it, they were just dangling there.
Poor, beautiful robots, swiveling on their wrists
to touch
to touch
useless
a blue empty bed
my outstretched arm

best to do nothing when panic drops its various poisons
down through the folds of my brain
it's not a *nest of vipers* that knots and spits at the base of this skull
otherwise I'd call you, to rescue them from me
to release them into the dark, safe grasses.

Snake-perception
that's what I wish for
locked up in this black room
wanting to grow a new organ, a new sense of smell
or to find something good in here: a band of warmth,
to feather up out of here on my ribs
the way a fern walks out of its tight spiral
an opening of green fingers.

This is for when your hands can do nothing
and it scares you
drowning straight down
embraced by an ocean of exhaustion.

Someone with wings is stroking the back of your head.
It is yourself
shut out by the gate of your spine.

All those bottles of little pills; echinacea
valerian, st john's wort, all the minerals for spiritual alchemy
zinc and incandescence, all the sacred letters: A and B, and F
and horny goat too, for christ's sake, and potent wood,
and a remedy for women
for the sorrowing Marys

I just want that bottle of little rattling deaths heads to stop up all the leaks
want to rattle down the hatches
and not come up

for air

but my lungs embrace the next breath
and the next one
you mean that cyclone was just
somebody breathing

The Dementia Ward

1.
Most of them are loveable now
being soft: clothes washed beyond colour
and shape.
They are mildly surprised when they find a shit
on the floor of their rooms.

They get the nurse.
No-one scolds them or judges them
they are beyond judging.
They left their habits of evil and good
in the rooms upstairs.

Family has fallen from them.
Guilt forgets to visit.
Hair, fragments of skin, the smell of leaves after rain
sift into corners and under cupboards
of fresh-washed clothes.

One calls out a woman's name that is not his wife's.
One has just stepped out of a plane.
Hans waits by the lift, which is always locked.
John Lee opens his mouth for the spoon.

2.
Zivaden

He told me he was Czech
but the nurses say he is Serbian.
It doesn't matter.
There's no-one here
who speaks his language.

If you aren't careful he will grab your arm
and say strange words to you
in Serbian, or Czech, or perhaps
in a new language.

Today he has been calling out across the creek
one great word.
It sounds like "HEYYYY..."

In this heat it is intolerable.
We want him to shut up
but he is heedless as a crow
and as unreadable.
                    He has bitten
some of the nurses.
He sleeps on any man's bed and his clothes
are the clothes of dead men.

In the laundry they rip off the names
and iron on this one:
Zivaden.

3.
A Question for Zivaden

Where do you go when your mind
goes inside you
somewhere small and unreachable
and intensely dark?
Or is it a dispersal,
molecules of mind rising, like water
from the surface of a dam.

Where does the mind go?
Does it break

is it suspired like breath
does it take the self with it?
Who are these men
shuffling through disinfected corridors and finding amazing things:
angels
slabs of human flesh
and keys.

4.
When you step out of the lift the doors lock behind you.
The trolley-wheels stick in the gap between the lift
and the floor.
Jugs of thickened fluid wobble
sluggish and sweet:
this is one of the levels of Hell.

Because surely only the most vicious of men
would deserve this.
To forget the name of his bride.
To be condemned to steal toilet rolls
from toilets forever restocked
by gentle nurses.
To repeat each day a conversation
about a key.

Prisoner of your body's good health
what did you do?
You don't remember.

and so you've become a shadow
wandering in dust
waiting for the living to bring you a sacrifice:
to bring you a cup of blood
so that you may drink, and wipe your mouth, and speak.

And then what questions I would ask you
and what truths you would tell
Zivaden
Heinz Shmalenburg
Marty Jordan

your hands trembling at your cups
of thickened cordial.

5.
Yves

Van Gogh lives here.
Hoederlin lives here.
Christopher Smart lives here.
Sappho was here, briefly,
and Sylvia
and Virginia:
just visiting.
This is a Home for Men.

Yves Baloche lives here
but refuses to eat at table.
Koalas, the Statue of Liberty,
Tawny Frogmouths and a Tour d'Eiffel are his companions
and guests. Naked women stretch behind plastic curtains,
rub coconut oil into their sunburnt breasts.
Merric Boyd hunches over his exercise book and draws
carving with coloured pencil
draws
the shapes of things all in beauty
draws
until the light surrenders

They all left pieces of things to be swiftly got rid of
the way Yves leaves pieces
of his remaining foot
amongst the bandages
and invites me to look
into the sizeable hole
where bones rest
inside rot a delicate yellow.

I know who lives here.
I look.

Days of heat

malignant, purposeless
grass crackling underfoot

magpies, currawongs,
stagger around with open beaks
even the air shrivels up

you can't love anything on a day like this
you are being nailed into the earth
they say the last war will be fought over water
they say the last war will be fought in a burnt-out field

you grab some things and put them in the car
you grab your child and put her in the car
you grab some books and some photographs
you grab some boxes and a basket of tangled threads

leave now
hurry
fire is stalking you

sirens and the beating of a giant heart

your bodies and their precious loads of water
are full of everything you left behind
fused into a tumour of plastic, charcoal, glass, metal, brick
you scream high velocity damaging winds

by evening the fire has been contained
the house has not collapsed
something tore inside you anyway
you cut and cut at snarling threads

China Creek

1.
All I want to be
is digging down by the creek.
Sifting the earth away
from children's faces and clay
teapots that shone in the morning
a hundred years last week.
Bottles that open their broken lips
to speak.

It's morning, shy rain fell last night
as the mopoke sang to the huddling clouds
It's alright. It's alright.

Joy is there in the soil
in the digging's deep play
and the settlers' eyes meet mine
as I brush the dust away.

2.
The year I begin to dig is the year the brush turkeys come
ringing each rung of the back steps softly
to inhabit the landing in instalments: a beak, a claw
a flicker of eye.
Shabby and wary they arrive in the kitchen
at cat biscuits and crumbs.

They have watched me on the bank
throwing dust up behind and pushing dead leaves away.
They know me.
They pick through my hillocks of knuckle-bones and oyster-shells
bubbles trapped in milky glass
grubby cheeks and ears

and shocked pink lips of dolls wept over
by antique children.
They keep an eye on me
when they go up to roost on sturdy branches
and my own eyes grope for the last glint of china.

The year the brush turkeys invite themselves in I begin to find birds
and pieces of birds in the earth: a kingfisher wing
a gold-beaked swan. Pheasants chase each other along the rim
of a tragedy – the best china dropped, or thrown
as turkeys hunt their rivals from my kitchen
brittle remnants of an age when birds stalked this delta
and the green earth shook.

3.
The creek is flowing like a river at the bottom of our garden. I am
sitting out on the grass. There is a small dark baby in my arms, or
perhaps the baby is floating down the river. She is in the water but
she is not drowning, and now I am holding her. Her back is lightly
and softly furred with dark hair. Her legs are splayed like a frog's. The
river washed her out of me and now she is the newest, softest thing
in the garden. I hold my arms around her, I protect her with my flesh
and my skeleton. She doesn't know that the garden is dangerous, she
doesn't know anything, she is sleeping. The river is carrying her away,
the water flows red and furious, the river spills over into the garden
but we are not drowning.

4.
glass Quan Ying

I said: 'Take her with you, she is the goddess of mercy and compassion'
and Miriam said: 'From now on her name is Ruth.'

On the back steps I talk to Miriam through the calm smile of Quan Ying
telling her what she has always known

that I birthed her the only way I could
I will hold her as long as I have arms
and I will let her go if I have to
but I will never let her go

5.

the river rips open the garden, dragging away trees
clawing up the footpath and thrusting through the road
crumbling the road through its fingers

the river brushes away street signs and white wooden fences
buses and bushes
garbage bins, besser blocks and outdoor furniture
stroking the figs' parched limbs

the river flushes out all its ticks and lice
all its sores and swellings
the river pulls pieces of the road along with it and flings them into houses
'fuck the po-lice, fuck the police,' yells the river
vandalising the playground
swallowing the tracks and the stations
carving its return to the sea

6.

In late November
we came up from the creek, ankles bleeding, socks bristling with burrs
out of the dark path of mud and rusting iron, fallen branches, tiny,
        poisonous black pools
with one piece of china in a blue plastic bag. Sophie spat on it and
    rubbed the grime away.

The creek is what they forgot, the settlers who made it a reliquary
for smashed eggcups black bedsteads gin jars and a ploughshare
too heavy for us to drag out of the slime.
The creek is what they took into consideration, the engineers

who drew up bridges and stormwater drains and roads,
and what they sold and are selling, the estate agents, to investors
who mark their boundaries in chickenwire and palms.

Untidy, disreputable, dirty
coughing up buttons and bones in wet weather
cupping mosquito larvae and toad eggs in black water
incubating fish eggs and worm eggs in rotten mud
snagging bottlenecks and horseshoes in roots and rocks
harbouring water dragons and brush turkeys, harbouring scavengers
the creek mutters its story to strangers and children
from a broken mouth.

When rain comes, water rushes like blood from an artery, thick with
    topsoil
          and rust
past the gardens and the nursing home, flattening papyrus, infant
    mulberry
          and grasses
squeezing through the tunnel under the road
half-river, half-drain
a man who wakes in a small room and for a few moments
remembers
exactly who he is

7.
losing it

am I a bad girl who does good things sometimes
or a good girl who does bad, goes mad
loses it, chooses it, chooses to lose it and throw it all away

children break like delicate vases
like glass under too much heat
like a cup thrown onto a stone

did I drop my daughter?

I confess that I have lost her, that she has left me
and the men on my street tell me stories
of leather straps and punches, of wooden spoons broken across arses
of cardboard beds and only the footpath to feed them
of heroin mothers, speed mothers and step-fathers
alcohol mothers and fathers
how did I break my daughter?

a child is not a knife
but what a sharp weapon she has been honed into
what a beautiful blade she is
in the hands that wield her
but a child is not a knife and the child is the flesh
that is wounded over and over

I open a bottle of red and the neck breaks in my hand
cutting my fingers, so I pour from the fracture and drink
to a child who is bottled up with poison
who is not a child
who is not a knife
who is my daughter

and I see him use her as a weapon and I let the blade tear through me
and I hold the child until her father comes to get her and drives her away

8.
and in the dust and pebbles of china creek are broken children.
their faces tumble out of the earth.
girls pouting or smiling, eyeless pink faces
and tiny white teeth.
a naked boy steps into a bath.
he is cold and his arms are wrapped around his chest
as he tests the water.

later the house will burn down and all his brothers and sisters
will be lost in the fire
but he tumbles out into the dust of china creek
where small boys and babies find dinosaur bones
where glass bottles swallow their cargo of earth
where wheels and lead soldiers are melded by heat
and toy guns rust to flaking fists

what's this? we ask, *what's this?*
thumbing the grime away
to see the children smile again
from the lip of a bowl or a chip of crazing china

'A Child Is Not a Knife': title of a book of poetry by Göran Sonnevi, Swedish poet,
published in 1993

Quan Yin: a goddess venerated in China, Korea and Japan

Shadow Daughter

To hold a grudge like that
to be so angry for so long
takes all your strength.

Very thin now, like a rock standing in the sea
you cast a shadow like a knife.
Like a knife you have cut away
anything that held you to me:
your family name, your family -
aunts and uncles,
cousins, grandparents - all excised.

Like Athene you spring full-grown
from your father's mind.

Look at you, standing in the ocean
staring away from land.
The horizon looks so empty
when you believe you are drowning
when you believe you are completely alone.

Your childhood is a secret locked in a shell.
I will keep it for you.
I will never sell it or throw it away.

For the shadow daughter, a shadow mother:
a shuffling beast.

In dreams I hear you, crying for me
crying —
but when I wake I have no arms
no hands
no face.

For Miriam

That night
all night
I sewed you a pair of wings
stretching white muslin over wire
coaxed into flight-shape:
the aspirations of a half-grown swan.

Selecting each feather
real swan feathers
plucked by your grandmother from the Avon's banks
and skimmed in a standard business envelope (recycled)
across the breadth of the continent.

Also the breast-feathers of sulphur-crested cockatoos
singing out at dusk from skyscraper gums
on the banks of the Ross River.
I wouldn't let you have the best ones, but here they are
tethered to muslin by white cotton thread
as the house breathes in
and the fig drops its leaves on our roof.

Night is cross-hatched by latticed wood and painted louvres.
We trust the paperbark, a flowering gum and spiny carpentarias
to watch over us, while dark swings in the aerial roots
of our elephant fig (snuffling its underground trunk
into wastewater.
Plotting its mighty treks through earth and across sky.)

This house believes that no one will harm us
that dust is an uninvited but distinguished guest
that only the clean-hearted can step onto its floorboards.

'Accept the cockroaches,' it counsels,
'nesting between the sheets of your drawings,
stripping gouache moths and orchids back to the blank page
and leaving only bright pellets of shit,
orange and petal-pink,
like miniature conceptual artists.
'Accept them, if not for their audacity,
then for the wet-ink eyes of the tree frogs
hunting all night in the sink.'

While the frogs stick themselves to pot-lids and say their grace
while the fig raps its tusks on the roof
while cockroaches fornicate under a postcard of Utamaro's
Six Renowned Beauties (Okita Geisha Girl)
while you rock in your dream-coracle,
I am sewing the last feather to its purchase of wire.

Only good things can come in now;
the rosella who pinned herself to the curtains
and shared your porridge for a week,
the man bright as morning
trusting as a hand-reared bird.
Tomorrow night he will be there
and you will wear your wings.

Whatever else you hold against me
in your black-and-white heart
remember I made them for you
even though they slipped from your shoulders
and they never flew.

1988

I kissed him goodbye at the airport
promising I'd come home, and we both cried.
I didn't know enough to know that it was over
but there was an itch in my bones
a sadness that was not about leaving.

What was I leaving?
A bedsit in a stack of grey units
a view of quartz-embedded clay
shod feet trotting down a back road.

Him smoking his exiled cigarette out front,
leaning his elbows on the concrete wall,
watching lights bloom in office blocks and penthouses.

It was a dress that everyone said suited me,
that he loved me in.

I started walking across the Bridge at night
walking fast past clocks and magazines and mannequins
stalking through the Gardens on stilts made of giant burned matches.

I was walking away from the bed in the corner
and a monitor humming blankly on Level Fifteen.
I did both jobs grudgingly,
grifted minutes from every shift.

Where is the life we lost while living? was not a question
that occurred to me, nor did I ask
why the friend I liked best was a book.

Two small accidents —
a thin brown spine in a secondhand shop on Castlereagh Street,

a clear, bright dream of a friend.
I woke up and bought a single ticket.

He kissed me goodbye at the airport and we both cried,
clutching onto promises I thought I would keep.
I cried again in my journal as the plane tracked the sun
over a long, narrow day,
a screen saver of ocean.

He was twenty. He wanted two babies
and I was nineteen.

The wheels touched down
on earth red and real
as the blood jumping through me

and every cell in me was shouting:
Africa!

Tehom, the Ocean Depths

(i)
Sad, lying, kind
you crouch on the earth, your back against a tree
and frangipanis inhale your smoke. We've just fucked, numbly
too angry with ourselves, and with those others
who didn't even bother to be there when they stabbed.
You'll knock on a vein, it'll open
the way I can't. Screwed tight around myself and whimpering.

(ii)
'Perhaps we could fall in love,' you say, as if you can just say 'fall'
as if it'd be a good idea. The hairs rise along the back of my neck. I'm
like a hungry cat
wanting to get to the foodbowl, shrinking under your hand.
'Why's your mouth so bitter?' I want to crawl right out of my skin.

(iii)
You stay the night. I can't sleep
with your finger inside me. I give you a bracelet; bronze,
made in Africa, I haven't taken it off my wrist for seven years.
'Is this the kind of gift you'll want back in a few week's time?'
Later your hand creeps back between my legs.

(iv)
'How do you orgasm with a broken clit?'
'Sure I'm sad about it, but you can't be sad for years.
It's like old water, it sinks under the skin.'
You drink from my nipples and after a while you tell me
that the top of your mouth is numb.

(v)
With my fingers and cupped hand
I trace the cup of sea

that we carry so cleverly
walking over this city. Only now
when you are lying down
does the sea spill over.

But the hard bubble of a pearl
is not in my hand now
this
sharp little triangle
this soft knife
this dorsal fin
well, you are neither oyster, nor rose.
But can I look at you again in daylight?

(vi)
Let's become a bell.
Let night curve over us. Let each star reverberate.
Don't move. My pelvis resonates
above your tongue. Let's kiss, let words spiral
from the soft holes in our skulls.
As if kissing were a forgotten craft
the ghost of lost wax in a temple bell.
Your smoothness
a lozenge I roll and cradle inside me.
Tehom.

(vii)
You kiss with your eyes open.
I'm not in love with you and the suggestion
doesn't taste like chocolate.
Your hands are dry, smoked to bloodlessness
although they never smell so yellow.
After you leave
my dress whispers about you; a warm perfume
and I cry until the red eyes of the clock say midnight.

(viii)

That day, the rockholes and the creek, such a female place,
water swelling from two narrow fountains
into a deep pool. On the way home, in the borrowed car
the baby asleep, the road movie theme-song
it wasn't you, I swear, it was the hills and trees
carrying away the sky behind your head.

(ix)

We are the loaded coin
the double-headed queen
of a nameless, familiar country.
Our borders constantly shift.
You drink my mouth.

(x)

I apologise for my breasts. The baby ate them.

(xi)

I wad sentences into the spaces between us.
In the dark I reach across and touch your cheekbone
your open eyes, your delicate, avian spine.
I explore the shape of us, and I know, now
why men are so afraid.

(xii)

They're zen breasts, you tell me. Your voice is dreamy, furred
by years of dope. 'I love you
almost as much as cigarettes.'
We give up, go outside, squat under the flowers.
I watch you breathe out complex poisons
I dream of planting a garden: datura, golden caps, cane toads and cannabis.
You could sit there till your skin glowed blue.
I love you almost as much as my fear.

(xiii)
'I ate a spider once. It was my suicidal phase.
Beth'd left me again. It was big as a bird, hairy.
I crammed it into my mouth and swallowed it
but nothing happened at all.'
'What did it taste like?'
'Skeletal.'

(xiv)
Look at you, rolling a cigarette, a fleck of white paper on your chin.
The ragged dreads, the T-shirt promised together by pins, the parched
    skin on your neck.
You smell of dry-season earth, and a creek nearby, under the sand.
You want to take the baby away for the afternoon, give me a break
but I can't let you, panic sculpts me hollow and thin.
When she's away I have nothing; I'm already broken.

(xv)
It's no good. I don't have the guts to tell you to your face.
You say 'Oh well,
I'll buy that car.' You give me your old bike, you insist you still love me.
'That woman, she takes you on such an amazing journey,' your good
    friends say.
But in the end, you don't say goodbye.

Good Night

Last night - was it only last night? - I drank myself ferociously drunk. A whole bottle. I didn't set out to drink, though it'd been a rough day. Just a glass, I thought. One golden glass of chardonnay, watered down with ice. One singing golden glass, after the scouring heat, the jolting bus-rides, the tired, nagging children, angry tired, too tired hot to sleep, too young hot tired to know it's not my fault. One glass...

It went down, like good loving, good human love, like falling into a good friend's arms, the loving intention of a kiss. Ice-kiss, little hard kisses, tipofthenose, tipofthetongue, little inquiries.

But I wasn't thinking of love, I was just thirsty. And the day was so rough, and plain; a hessian day, dutiful, thrifty. There was a new bottle in the fridge, slendergreen crisp as a pear. A week-and-a-half's worth of goodnight kisses.

I drank myself drunk, ferociously, because of a little kiss. A little kiss undid me, like a bag with a broken zip. A bag corded shut with a long piece of orange nylon, tugged and twisted into bunchedup knots, uncommitted nylon, slipperyblind as a promise. Just a little twitch and the cord slips off, the bag flips open, clean clothes and dirty knickers clutter the bitumen, clip-clop feet step around me. But there are no feet. No strangers to glance away, no thief to snatch a shirt or buckle. Just me, and a bottle, and a kiss.

They were laughing, they smelt each other's quiet smell and they liked it. He was greybalding; a little stubble suited him; she was dazzling, slightly mad; mouth like a violin solo. I knew him, the thirst in his throat, his mouth moving in, how she answered him, hummingquiet and lovely.

I could see closeup the back of his head, the fine skin, her kiss pulling him forward, her music opening, kissing him back. It was uglyplausible, all the little coloured dots resolving into fine grey hair his wrinkled neck his tentative irresistable tenderness. Again they kissed.

I drank I drank I gluttoned. Ice curled into my tongue, my

throat melted my belly filled up warm and golden. You'll regret
this in the morning I promised and wrung out the ice-tray, ran
my tongue around the bottom of the glass. Here's to love, here's to
goodwarmloving, and the polished floor received me, his chest with
the finefrailsweetstrong skin of an old man curved to receive me, like
a promise, like sleep.

Being

for Paul

I conceived that first night we lay together
when you offered yourself to me,
pressing gently against my back
and I turned around on the bed
to kiss you

Later, as I drank you
something began in me: an almost imperceptible
heartbeat

I knew the symptoms: crying in the bath
and at any sudden beauty –
the flash of wings, a smell of growth
in the breeze.

At three months, I was afraid I'd lose it
the child budding in me. There was a day spent
huddled over the cracks in the floor.
But you were back by evening...
my hands stopped shaking...

Seven months.
Something that belongs to both of us
turns inside me
has your hands, my face.

Almost viable.
Almost
a being I can trust.
Although I know how dangerous it is.
How difficult the last few hours
must be.

After the Ultrasound

A daughter.
The strangeness of it:
another girl.

My first-born is sixteen
wary as an antelope
tearing her head away from my hand

away from where her sister wakes now to fluid morning
the dark engine room where the placenta
beats a slow underscore to her rushing heart.

She doesn't know me
yet all she knows is me
my body her burgeoning self
limbs brushing against our shared wall
voices of family rippling
through amniotic sky.

As the careful heat of ultrasound picked her out
in star-pricked black and white
as her bones were measured, her organs mapped
her blood followed through the chambers of a ship-shape heart

I watched her father
fall through intricate architecture
the skull, the fists, the thrusting legs
of his first child

and I saw him arrive at love

A Definition of Bliss

Time. A friendly chair. Rain-light greening the room.
Time untold by the critical clock or busybody machines.
Time, cold and hard and clean
as seashells and bracelets of kelp in a stone bowl.
Under the window a child reads,
belly stretched along the woollen rug
and her arms around the neck of a black panther.
Black leaves,
the forest floor,
the silent spring.
Against her hand the great heart beats.
Hot thick fur against her cheek.

Time. Grey Sydney sandstone, quartz-beaded and cooled
by lemon-scented leaves.
Two green apples fished from a canvas bag
and polished on your duds.
We swing our legs over the cliff, a seventy-year old boy
and a girl of twenty
sharing apples and silence.

A long white beach and the waves' black hiss.
Lights on the headland.
Lights on and a table set in the heartland.
Sleeping fish lifted and set down by every wave.

Time. Time without minutes or hours
rain-drums heard from a big dry bed
long after the book has been closed,
the lover brought to bliss,
held now in the slow black wave of his breath.

Requiem for an Orphan

in memoriam Reginald Edward Edwards, 1922 – 2000

i.
The curlews are crying all over Tokyo.
In the streets of Mita and Azabu
they are spreading aboriginal wings.
They are opening their yellow mouths
in the night streets of Shibuya.
They are crying and crying
staring from white-rimmed eyes
spreading the white tips of their feathers.
They are dancing for you
dancing your death
in the night streets of Tokyo.

ii.
This is for the faceless father who dandled your half-brothers
and half-sisters
on his knee in a small flat in London.
This is for the widow, planting a child
in a holy garden.
I repent, she wrote
of my sin.
This is for her eldest daughter
faithful Nell
who Never Told.
This is for a wicked baby, with a dubious surname
smiling up at strangers
who called him *son.*

Were you happy there
transplanted
to parents and a brother
not related to you by blood?

Did you hear the curlews of England
calling to you in the fields?
Did you know what they prophesied?
Did you know they danced for you?

iii.
This is a story of names: Clarke,
Church, and maybe Edwards —
honest English names to work in factories
and parlours and beetfields
(though he had curly black hair and a hook nose,
that Joseph
who cuddled a dead man's children on his lap)

The second time you died
you were eleven. A car came for you and your brother.
The letter came first, to sever you from your inheritance: a field in Sussex,
a box of toy soldiers,
the farmers Clarke.
They had told them from the beginning,
the authorities — told them that these babies
were the property of England
and would be sent for.

How could the woman you called *mother* stand at the door
and wave you goodbye?
How could your father stand in the road
and wave you goodbye?

The curlews cried from the fields
defending their huddled young
but the sound was the sound of something breaking:
the ice-cold hinges of the world.

iv.
At your third death
I met your foster-brother Ken.
We talked quietly in the waiting room.
This tall, thin old man
with the silk tie and the fortune in handbags
told me one of the stories
from your kitchen.
In his soft mouth, without the chop-chop of your knife
it was a stranger's account of intimate grieving.
I was shocked at what he knew.
I'll put them away for you, Mother said,
In the cupboard over the stairs.
They would always be there. It was a promise.

In the recovery ward, having been two days dead,
you dipped thin slices of toast
in a soft-boiled egg
and Uncle Ken wore a bolder tie.
'Thirty years later
I went back to the house
and asked them living there
for the box of soldiers.
But no-one'd seem them.
It was like they'd never been.'

v.
They shipped them by the crate
those lost soldiers, to giant foster-children: Australia,
South Africa and British Canada
separating pairs sometimes,
by half a world.
Perhaps they looked the same
in their stifled, leaden silence.

In the photos of course they all look like Oliver
shaven heads and soupbowls
outrageously asking for more.
There's Ken, leaning further out over the table than any other boy.
That's my great-uncle.
I am linked to him by a story.

vi.
There are no photos of the boy who will be my grandfather.
There are no photos of his father, or his foster-parents.
Instead, I pick up stiff, grey images in secondhand bookshops:
a woman with deepset eyes. A child with large, square hands.
Strays from the albums of dead strangers
survived by no-one.
                    The childless Clarkes
take the letter from its bitter envelope. This picture of the boy
and his brother was taken by Alice, as she stood at the door and waved.
It is blurred by the movement of the car and her tears.
If it had been developed onto paper it would be meaningless,
but she kept it with her, inside her, and it never lost its sharpness.

vii.
The Stories.
I can tell them by heart.
They have come down to me
as an inheritance.
They, and his square hands,
are what I have.

I want to write an elegy but everything sours.
Rage twists each line.
It is his rage
as he held the knife in the kitchen
and chopped up carrots like they were responsible for it all:
the policies, the placements,

the ships, the separations.
The letters from Alice Clarke
that he never saw.

ix.
There are things that bewilder me. Your disgust at single mothers.
Your loyalty to the queen of bloody England.
England! - that cuckoo-mother depositing her eggs in others' nests
disembowelling other people's babies.
The way you grew, crabbed and strange like a tree that was blasted
before it could anchor itself in a field, but still growing, still reaching out
into air.
The way you cut Ken off like a tree that could hack off its own branches.
Your contempt of bastard Poms.

There were so many things you never told me
in that kitchen you raised up around your wife and children
that was solid as your love
that was the good work of those quick and thrashing hands.
Why did you hit them?
With your fists and with the leather shaving strop
and with words like metal and steam against the soft skin of children?
After you hit them
How did you teach them to love you?
How does a man remember some stories forever, like scars,
forget others like bruises?

ix.
The Kitchen.
My cousin buys it and the garden and both houses:
the Bottom and the Top.
Buys the grey sandy soil and forty years of tealeaves
and the roots of ancient rhubarbs and the bones of a host of cats
all named Cheetah.
Buys the foundations of the outdoor dunny

and the woodpile
and the workshop with its rack of screwtop jars and the doorjamb
carved with a child's heiroglyphics.
Buys the concrete ramp and the besserbrick wall and the hills hoist.
He tears out the kitchen benches that our grandfather built
from salvaged timber, planed and polished and solid as a reef.
Splintered wood and vinyl bolsters are carted away in skips.
Tasman, youngest of my uncles, scribe of doorjamb heiroglyphics,
    watches from his house
across the road.
In the green aquarium light of intensive care
I saw him shave his father's jaw and comb his hair
with a white comb, talking to him softly
in a voice warm as the day outside the coma-heavy room.

My cousin is renovating with the skills that are his gift from our
    grandfather.
My uncle sees his father, butchered and scattered amongst splinters of
good wood. He picks out a chipped eggcup from the rubble in the skip.
My cousin is developing his Property.
My uncle is witnessing a Desecration.
Neither of them are wrong.
Nails shriek in the wood.

x.
I wrote to him
from the week I learned how
from a childhood of country towns, and little cities,
and pacific islands.
He kept all our letters, photographs and drawings
in their envelopes, in a box.
I was writing to him in my room in Tokyo
the week he died. I wanted to tell him
how the conifers in the parking lot below me
had sprouted hard yellow buds, like candles.

My father brought them back after the funeral; a patchy
autobiography
in a shrinking hand. I smiled at the paintings I'd remembered as
wonderful.

Nineteen years, Grandpa, since I've written you a letter.
I had to dig out the yellowed envelopes
to check the number of your house.

Coda

Guardians of the dead, tell me where he is —
has he become the seabird he intended
is he flying on grey wings over grey seas
is he peaceful?
Are the dreams I have
of him locked in a dark room, in pain
and not remembering his own name —
are they just dreams?
In that last year
he died hard, he died slowly
piece by piece.
Guardians of the dead, you tell me
is he at ease now
is he flying low over cold grey seas?

R.E. Edwards was one of the 'Lost Children of the Empire'. Fostered out by the
Barnados Brothers to a loving couple (the Clarkes), he was taken from them at the
age of 11 and sent to Western Australia as a Fairbridge Farm labourer. Foster brother
Ken Church, aged 9, was sent to Molong in NSW. They did not see their foster parents
again, nor had word of each other until they met by chance as grown men.

Yesterday Today and Tomorrow

Last night I dreamed of the house on Pacific Street. I was naked,
walking through rooms owned by strangers. 'This was my room,' I
told the woman who was anxious for me to leave. Her three children
played in the garden, the way we three had played, leaping from the
verandah over yesterday, today and tomorrow, breathless that we had
jumped so far.

The books and mess of foreign children littered the floors but nothing
was very different; the weatherboard walls were still pink and
powdery as chalk. I rummaged through sheets in the linen cupboard
and showed her how my father had lined our bedrooms with egg
cartons: 'That was back when you could still do these things.' She
edged me to the hallway and I saw that the front door still wore its
doorknob; a large plastic ship.

It was good to have seen it, that pink shell fading in sunlight. It was
good to step into the shower and wash the salt from my arms. The
house remembered me. I would have liked to have stroked it, like a
loving old cat, but the woman began hosing off her children in the
driveway.

Someone lived there before us and someone lived there after but it
was ours, always, and the lookout, and the hairy armpit tree-ferns and
the dugout road down to the sea. Just a hedge, just a shrub really, that
we clenched our courage to jump over, rolling green-skinned onto a
summer lawn.

Becoming Human

This morning, with all the gravitas
of nearly six, you told me: 'Love never changes.'
You held my hand as we crossed the road. Rain hatched the raucous
  flight
of cockatoos: 'Sulphur crested,' you added. You like knowing things,
so do I, but I'm not as sure as you about the consistency of love.
I didn't tell you that, feeling the flex of hand and finger muscles
inside mine, hearing the crunch of our footsteps on the road.
'That's why I will always love you,' was what I said, and know for certain
with a lucidity that could x-ray bone, or measure the skull capacity
of the child now called Selam, three years old and dead three million
  years.
'How did she die?' you ask, over the rapture of paleo-neurologists
discussing the deep channel or crease found in the brain of a chimp
but not in Australopithecus Afarensis, nor in Homo Sapiens Sapiens
'the cleverest animal in the world' we like to think.
On the screen last night a hairy avatar of Selam trotted beside her tribe
of upright-walking not-quite-apes, put out a broad-thumbed hand and
  squeaked
(the hyoid bone unmodified for speech).

Having downloaded the file, a friend
printed out a copy in 3D of Tuang child's skull
grooves in the sockets of the eyes
torn when a raptor swooped and bore away
the wailing infant.
All I could think of was the Bidjara legend
of the Goori-Goori bird, and then there's Zeus and
Ganymede of Western dreaming, or the story told
in whispers by the skeleton of Ebony
much, much closer to home.

They will emerge, crowning from the desert,
the mushroom nubs of skulls and femurs,
six million, seven million years since deviation
from a common ancestor with genus Pan
to this rainy morning as we walk to school
a juvenile and adult *wise wise man.*

Selam, partial remains of an Australopithecus Afarensis female child discovered in
Ethiopia in 2000, about 3.3 million years old

Lunate sulcus: a fissure in the occipital lobe of monkeys and primates which shows a
marked decrease in size in hominid skull-casts developing towards genus *Homo*

Tuang child, Australopithecus Afarensis skull discovered in South Africa in 1924,
about 2.5 million years old

To print out a 3D copy of the reconstruction of the Tuang child's skull go to www.
radiolab.org/story/tuang-child/

Pan paniscus and Pan troglodytes, scientific names of the Bonobo and Common
chimpanzees

Ebony, or Baby Ebony as she is known, died in Adelaide in 2011, aged 4 months.
Examiners found 70 fractures on her body, inflicted by a beating from the baby's
father.

The Boat of Punjulharjo

That year he gave me a coastline for my birthday. I trailed the edge
of my sarong in the brimming water. Each morning, while he was
sleeping, I went to see what the sea had brought me. Coral lumps
coughed up by storm-waves and the grinning lips of conches, cowries
winking like eyes. High up in the sand I found a boat: a long, ribbed
outline, a sketch in stone-grey wood. A blanket of silt peeled back by
men cutting a new saltern from that bitter land, the liminal, the boat
rising up like a word in a forgotten language, spoken in a dream.
Fourteen hundred years dead, the boat-builders beckoned to me with
hands of plaited rope. They spoke to me in their language, pleased
that I had come up to them, coaxing me as if they knew me for a
strange, shy bird. I trusted them to carry me from island to island,
the centuries lashed together with sturdy cords, their eyes shining
like pieces of polished shell. I looked down through still water. Time,
fourteen hundred years of it, flowed around the timber, the coast of
Punjulharjo, the boat-builders' hands, into my rib-cage, into the rib-
cage of the boat. A stone face, a broken goddess, eyes narrowed against
corrogated sky. Then we were gone out of that moment in the sun.
A calf lifted its head as we drove by, tugging at weeds on a swollen
mound.

Nikko;
Almost Like Love at First Sight

To Set Out on a Journey

Why do people travel? From time immemorial many have recounted their travel experiences: journeys in quest of poetic contemplation, journeys in pursuit of spiritual discipline, journeys undertaken out of a sense of despair.
Shinno Toshikazu

The jizo by the roadside will smile after you.
You may stop to pray to him
to breathe in his smell of incense and darkness.

Ksitigharba, who came to the dying Buddha
with a promise.
Guardian of unborn children, pregnant mothers,
and travellers,
the Japanese call him Jizo, and love him.
He smiles from the crossroads, from beside railways,
on busy street corners.

When you go to Japan, you will meet him
a stone monk dressed in a red cotton bonnet and a bib.
By his feet a small stuffed animal
darkens with city dirt and rain.

He is a comforter
of those in distress
lost wayfarers and parents
of lost children
a stone standing up out of the desire to ease suffering
as human as the other desire
to cause it.

Never desecrated, never stolen
those eyes that have watched so many shoulders
set to so many roads.

Nikko, Early Spring

If I ask myself what am I doing here
why did I come here:

to listen to the river running black and clean outside my window
to walk on frozen, day-old snow.
To be in a world where the dominant tones are monochrome:
black trees springing leafless from white ground
chocolate, russet and rust of the mountains
forests of *sugi* rising above shadow.

To be lonely
to think with my feet
to be always moving

to learn that the dragons on the roof of the *Karamon* can't fly away
because their fins and tails are clipped.
To pray for true love, and a happy marriage, at the shrine of bridging.
To stare into the Daiya River, where it is green as flourite, and so clear
rust-coloured leaves turn in the current like fish.

To walk through streets patchworked with old and new Japan,
ancient mountains slashed by telegraph wires
the stars undimmed, unbroken.
To say good morning to a woman at her doorstep
warming her tiny, brittle body in the sun.

To walk in a holy place
to journey on foot up a mountain.

To learn that there are beasts that eat dreams
and beasts that breathe mirages
and guardian-deities that eat the tribulations of humankind.

To hear a stone crying.
To follow paths through books, through histories and legends
through fragments that visit me in dreams:

three women: mother, daughter, and grandmother
sharing a futon for warmth in deep winter
in a village lost in snow, in a house lit only by a lantern

To make drawings.
To look into the eyes of a wild deer.
To listen.

If you can, go to Nikko in early spring

when the last snows are still falling
when the neat, cloven hoof of the deer
is printed on the white slopes
and the dark rocks ache like iron
under your hand.

The mountains stare down, white and impassable.

Go when the gods are still up there in the mountains.
Before the river swells with melting snow
before the rice-fields thaw.

Cross the stone footbridge, in iron-hard evening
and find the jizo ranked by the river
moss frozen on their faces
and the last snow in their laps.
Climb the ice-slick path
above their heads.

If you can, go to Nikko when the tombs in that shadowed forest
stand up out of untrodden whiteness
their stones mottled grey and black
cracked china cups at their bases

when the blood of the shot deer is trapped in red crystals
by the tree-roots above the pool
whose stream hangs in silent curtains
of black and white glass.

Then you feel them staring
from out of the white sky
impartial to your belief
or your attention:
the cold mountains

they pull you, heavy as moons

Cold Mountain

Cold Mountain
is as much a state of mind
as a locality
        Arthur Waley

Kanzan.
Say it.
The name itself has ice in it.

Is barbaric
as the black voice of the earthquake

You can't go there
in thermal underwear
with a hot dinner under your jacket

you can't climb there
not with claws on your boots
not with chains on your tyres

you have to pull yourself up there
by your fingers
you have to hear the sob
in the stone

Cold Mountain.
I don't pretend to have seen it.
I sit with the men who are smiling at its base.
They had to step out of their bodies to get there.

My womb is full of books
with words that take the skin from my fingers
and my eyes are the colour of earth.

A long time ago I read about the sage of Cold Mountain
now I trace his features
with my living hand.

Narabi Jizo

when one died
his brothers carved his likeness in blue granite

some are straight-backed, some lean forward
meditating on emptiness
their cupped hands empty
despite snow, and offerings of coins, and frozen leaves

seven hundred, eight hundred years
they have sat in perfect zazen
in this dark place, on the bank of the river

they take no notice
of the changing dress of pilgrims
of blizzards, wars, or floods

some have lost their heads to giant waters
and some have been swept away, back to the river
to meditate face down in sand

men who devoted themselves
to the praise of the jewel in the lotus,
they must have laughed sometimes
and dived into the freezing waters of the Daiya
in high summer
when cicadas beat their waves of sound from bank to bank

and some few must have found it hard to concentrate
because under the lowered lids, stone eyes
have grown perfect irises of lichen, black and green
to glance sideways at the feet and hems of travellers

others pray so hard
you can still hear them, mumbling in their deepwater voices
nam myoho renge kyo

praying until the moss has furred them
until their faces have crumbled away

Nam myoho renge kyo: Glory to the Dharma of the Lotus Sutra

Spring Festival

They were wild, the old gods; they liked parties
o *matsuri*, with even the school teachers falling down
in stages of divine intoxication
and people keeping themselves warm
by lighting fires in their gut with rice wine
waiting at frozen midnight for the floats to come by
and the god-houses, the *mikoshi*, carried on sweating shoulders
all voices raised in wordless chant

the gods have come!
the gods have come down from the mountains!
to dance with their people in the fields
and if there was a little blood spilt, as well as *sake,*
if a police station or two was stoned
or a matron collapsed in the street, well
 there was a precedent for such things:

On Mount Tsukuba where eagles dwell
        By the founts of Mohakitsu,
I will seek company with others' wives,
Let others woo my own...

"Festivals these days
aren't what they used to be,"
the old folk mutter, and it's true
that the floats are too gorgeous
to be smashed against each other
that the young men no longer carry them straight into the sea
(the water being too polluted)
there are more tourists than youths
in shrinking villages
but the gods still come, you can feel them
their huge hearts beating in the drums

you can smell them, in the fires and incense
and the running sweat.

Even in Tokyo
the rich rice land calls up through subways forty stories deep
and a salary man on his way to work
stops at a construction site
to crumble friable soil in his hands.

This is the Greenwood

This is the greenwood.
This is what I've read about
or heard of, in the old songs
and stories.

This is where monkeys come;
here are their footprints in the damp, dark earth
here are their droppings, enriching the soil.

These are wild cherries, blossoming ancients
these are cedar, and these: red pine
red as salmon gums but rough-barked
and cripple-branching.

This is the greenwood.
These are daffodils: I never knew
their stems would be so fleshy
their perfume so deep and rich.

Early morning, and the trees shiver in their deep green hides
shaking out new leaves, scattering blossom

and everywhere the smell of earth coming alive
the little birds I have no names for singing
to their nestlings of the millenium of spring
they have lived and loved in, in this country.

This is the greenwood
this is the delicate light of spring
and somewhere, the knocking of branch on branch
and the colourful cries of crows.

Last Day in Nikko

and I'm still finding secret, sacred places
in the mountains.

Next to the supermarket carpark
a stone gateway
entrance to the other world.

No one has come this year to cut down the dandelions
or shovel black leaves from the steps.
Only crows draw oracles of garbage from swollen green bags.
Who has time these days
to read the slow, strange intelligences of the gods?

I leave the sunlight behind on a staircase of lichen-etched stone.
Now each step is cut into black earth, planked and pegged.
Will they be waiting for me in a clearing,
will I meet them in the eyes of a wild deer?

Where their houses huddle low and dark
the path pauses and invites me to choose:
climb into the mountains
or catch a train to Tokyo this afternoon.

Did I think
that the gods would come and greet me
at the gate?

While there is still time
I make the first steps of a journey
that will take me the rest of my life.
Then the gods in their laughing absence
watch me turn back and descend
into ordinary light

Train Journey: Nikko to Tokyo

Everything is alright when I'm on the train
lulling me, lulling me to sleep
old men and old women eating their lunches
talking softly
the train talking softly too
rocking slightly from side to side

Everything is alright, the tractors
in the paddy by the tracks
churning the drowned, brown soil
mountains peering over to look at themselves in silver mirrors.
Then the little towns, quiet and blind,
a woman walking her dog
and the cherry and plum in bloom.

Everything is alright; we are moving
busily knitting the miles between Nikko and Tokyo.
My needs are simple
I have my ticket in my pocket.
And the train rocking side to side is lulling me
as the towns become larger, the railway bells more insistent
the cedar fewer, smaller.

A journey of four days
on a pony in straw sandals
when spring summoned drowsy nobles
to the capital on the plains

beyond the mountains drowning in their fields
beyond the tiny claws of the maple, opening in trust
to wake up in the city
to wake up in another world.

Plague Animals

1985

I cried when I first saw Tokyo
coming in on the airport bus
with the other Australians.

I couldn't believe that humans had created
something so desolate
a place where nothing could live
nothing except plague animals: rats, and crows
and people.

I cried because I could not see one tree
from the concrete flyover
because dusk was a nightmare of fairylights
pink and yellow, orange and green
stabbing me from steel hexagons and rectangles
studded with glass.
Because the entire vista was an accusation: *this is what it comes to
you clever,*
clever monkeys.

All my muddy rivers, all my pebbles and clay
were stomped into a papier-mâché grey of angles and corners.
The filthy wind had nothing to stroke it, no hills,
no branches.

Like a small animal in a comfortable cage
I huddled and wept
while the city kids and the bush kids – all strangers –
chatted and craned and seemed excited
seemed not to notice
where we were.

At Yoshinoya

where a meal costs less than a postcard to Australia
I order: a large warm bowl of greyish rice
strips of grey beef laced with rainbow
and a raw egg to stir in with my chopsticks.
The skinny, pimply student hiding behind the rice-cooker
is glad when I can ask for it in Japanese.

Poor people come here, young men in worker's overalls
and grey-haired, stubble-faced elders
from the cities of cardboard.
It's bright
in the 24 hour popmusic
we come for the posters which say "Treat us like family!"

Strangers, we slurp and chew without speaking.

My favourite moment is when I call out "Gochisosama!"
and get out my 300 yen. My fingers brush
against his thin palm.
This, and the rice
gets me through the day.

Acknowledgements

Some of these poems have been published in the following:
Blue Dog, Soft Blow, Big Bridge, Blast, Papertiger, The Second Rule; New Music, An Anthology of Contemporary Australian Poetry; The Force that Through the Green Fuse Drives the Flower and *The Puncher and Wattman Anthology of Australian Verse.*

The Nikko poems were written with the assistance of an Australia Council individual project grant. 'The Exile of the Imagination' was written during a Bundanon Trust residency, and a Varuna fellowship enabled me to work on the manuscript in its entirety.

Thank you Paul and Amelia for love and support always. To Rosemary and Tony for their encouragement and comments on the poems, and to my sister Elizabeth for close reading and comments on several drafts of the manuscript over the years. Thank you to Gina Mercer, Leonie Tyle, Cyril Wong, Felix Cheong, Yong Shu Hoong, Kunitaka Yoneyama, Takuya and Keiko Suzuki, Brett Dionysius, Melissa Ashley, Jeanie and John Adams, Robert Barton and Suzy Gilmour for support – including paid work! -at crucial times in my development as an artist and poet, and to Dimity Knight and Jann Makepeace for feedback and friendship since moving to Adelaide. Thank you to my host family, Hori Katsumi, Yuri, Yuko and Kyoko, for looking after a sixteen year-old girl from Katherine and teaching her to love Japan. Finally, many thanks to Martin Langford and David Musgrave of Puncher and Wattmann for their comments and editorial advice, and for publishing this collection.